THE SEVENTY PREPOSITIONS

NEW CALIFORNIA POETRY

EDITED BY	Robert Hass
	Calvin Bedient
	Brenda Hillman

CAROL SNOW

THE SEVENTY PREPOSITIONS

POEMS

UNIVERSITY OF CALIFORNIA PRESS
BERKELEY   LOS ANGELES   LONDON

University of California Press
Berkeley and Los Angeles, California

University of California Press, Ltd.
London, England

©2004 by The Regents of the University of California

For acknowledgments of permissions, please see page 109.

Library of Congress Cataloging-in-Publication Data

Snow, Carol, 1949–
    The seventy prepositions : poems / Carol Ann Snow.
        p.   cm. — (New California Poetry ; 10)
    Includes bibliographical references (p.).
    ISBN 0-520-24077-4 (alk. paper).
    ISBN 0-520-24081-2 (pbk. : alk paper)
        1. Rock gardens, Japanese—Poetry.   2. Ryōanji (Kyoto,
Japan)—Poetry.
    I. Title. II. Series.
PS3569.N57S48   2004
811'.54—dc22   2003061616
                                                        CIP

Manufactured in Canada
13   12   11   10   09   08   07   06   05   04
10   9   8   7   6   5   4   3   2   1

The publisher gratefully acknowledges the generous contribution to this book provided by the General Endowment Fund of the University of California Press Associates.

CONTENTS

THE SEVENTY PREPOSITIONS

VOCABULARY SENTENCES

So, before I could go on and write my story, I had to jot down
various words for the names of objects, things, phenomena, ideas.
I'd write these down whenever they came to me. Then I'd take
the words, sentences, and ideas I'd collected in this way and
begin to write my story in a notebook, regrouping the words and
sentences, comparing them with others I'd seen in books. Finally
I managed to write a sentence expressing an idea I had for this
story of my illness.

FROM THE DIARIES OF L. ZASEYSKY
A.R. LURIA, *THE MAN WITH A SHATTERED WORLD*

BIT

'A slight'

sounded.

Reverberating—in what box?—or reiterated
—like a booster shot, like the roosters in Bishop—
    sustained

(this illustrated by my tilting half a glass of orange
    juice
up over an empty glass—"I'm a little teapot . . .";
more precisely: The Mystery Spot, "Cannons ready!"
    horizon to the rim, *the extreme verge*,
surface tension [J. knew a word for it]—pouring

[not spilling, by virtue of the empty glass, not
    threatened]
suspended), suspended.

One survived—a part of her part of a part of the story
replaying in excerpts in the Holocaust Museum—the
    forced, then called a Death,
March through the dead of winter among thousands,
    among hundreds, by spring, tens,
of three young women struggling abreast, arms linked
    so that in turn,
the one in the middle could sleep. 'The whole for
    a part'

then 'a part for the whole,' her visage, *a certain
    Slant of,*
quote, what a bell

meant (the sound of [J. would know the word]—
  'synecdoche'), *so one of us could sleep.*

Heard (as thought)
but also spelled (?!): 'a slight'

—not yet insult, minor, a slip of a

VOCABULARY SENTENCES

1. are

Some <u>are</u> saved and some <u>are</u> drowned.

2. during

Would he hold my hand <u>during</u> it?

3. local

The effect—<u>local</u>—of sorrow on the flavor of pudding.

4. satisfied

After twelve years of marriage, her curiosity was
<u>satisfied</u>.

VOCABULARY SENTENCE(S)

1. grimace

Was vocabulary in the <u>grimace</u>?

                                   a slight
grimace or hint of a leer I called a grin, it seemed
     absolutely
internal (of the 'subtle

body'—I presumed, unsuspected) though also an
     imposition . . .

As when placing the (roof of the) tongue on the roof
     (but, the ceiling)
of the mouth, the sensory the subjective inter- (or is
     it intra-?) mural . . .

A child pretending to sleep imagines being seen—
    what (trace of) 'steals over'
her features?—who's there? (The angel of the
    Assumption?)

Self-conscious (unevenly).

I'd like to introduce my dissociate, ——.

Our little triumphs.

"Yes, things are going very well, I think." As in,
    someone else's misfortune. As in, 'taking in.'
    As in, taken into confidence.

(Faintly) smirking or sneering, superior? self-
    mocking. Self-satisfied (unevenly).

He said, "Show me. Exaggerate."

    —From inside the chapel, we'd glimpsed the
      structural additions.
    —The expression (quite pleasant, utterly
      unfamiliar) someone gave my father's cadaver.
    —Seeing only the backs of those hoisting the staves
      of the banner we marched behind.
    —I thought I recognized, in the yanked bowing
      of the actress's mouth, in her scaffolding of
      building up to weeping—

Though also an interposition . . .

"—That looks more like a wince, really."

CONVERSION ("SPIN")

That same self-consciousness,
on nearing the sink . . . studied . . . an expression
itself not 'studied' or 'affected'—the inadvertent slight
upward plying in my lips—civil . . .

affected. Not entirely unlike—is it?—rather bearing
    some resemblance to,
conversant with, akin to the "dawning" of (why
    shameful?)
joy on the face of an approached, recognizing
lover?

VOCABULARY SENTENCES

1. play

A hand puppet showed "trying to escape"

—wrist, forearm, elbow,
upper arm, shoulder:—

<u>play</u>.

2. betray

—and woke from a reverie of conflation, half-
missing now: glib prologue then Dog Boy
as the Elephant Man. I was, for whatever reason,
loath to <u>portray</u> my happiness.

ALSO TO ILLUSTRATE

At a table in the bookstore's café
after the "Poetry and Motherhood" reading (five of
    the six of us:
women, writers), one's "wordless bond" with her five-
    year-old daughter—
"May I take your order?"—then stories about
    wordlessness.
(Aphasia, Alzheimer's, insult to the brain . . .)

                    For the moment the Stevie Smith
forgotten, I recounted, vaguely . . .

[success! since I'd not, as yet, purchased *The Man with
    a Shattered World:*

The History of a Brain Wound— one of two Lurias
    borrowed and read—
expressly to relinquish the particulars of his anguish.

Listen:

He had to hunt for a word and sort through dozens
of others he turned up along the way, just as people
do when they are searching for a name they've
forgotten. He would try to find the class to which a
word belonged and substitute too broad a category
("It's . . . an object . . . a thing . . . an animal . . .").
He tried to find some sort of context that might
help him think of a word ("But you see . . . they
smell so good . . . these red, beautiful, fragrant . . .
roses!"). He tried automatically to evoke what he
could not remember at will, but only succeeded at

times, though he resorted to every conceivable
device in that world of deranged probability.]

And heartlessly reconstruing,
(*beyond name and form;* well, beyond . . . without
    name: why wasn't he very very
happy?)—"Could I taste your biscotti?"—

largely misquoting his affliction,
[listen—from the diaries the subject called "I'll
    Fight On!":—

After I was wounded, I just couldn't understand
space, I was afraid of it. Even now, when I'm sitting
next to a table with certain objects on it, I'm afraid
to reach out and touch them.

and listen:

> . . . I can't even recall the words for things in my
> room—things like *closet, cupboard, blinds, curtains,*
> *window sill, frame,* etc. . . . And when I go for a long
> time without being able to remember and *train*
> myself to use these words in speaking, I forget what
> things I see are called; I pay no attention to them.]

employing a 'meaningful gaze' or 'intent look,' and
   relying—
far, in that, from my almost certainly disquieting
   post-adolescent "Don't ask but please guess"
   semaphore with restaurant condiments—
I raised—displayed—the

. . . I tried to say to . . . someone that I could not
find the word I wanted. But instead of 'word' I said
'milk' first & then 'snow.'

—Stevie Smith, on her stroke

. . . meaning: *Just this, among us, dear friends.*
And meaning . . . —Of course, I can't speak for them.

TRACE

I mean, really: teaching children 'words' for the
    sounds animals make.

"Report on B____." "Illustration,"
a tracing of its coastline.

(Most of the coves were invention.)

Learned my portion.

Was apt.

Apt to lean, near as pinna to tympanum,
to the netted speaker slots of the Emerson hi-fi (I'd
     arrived —
first? — at sibling rivalry) smugly
already to have mastered Dad's newest Broadway cast
     album.

(Mastered, largely: lyrics, most melody, an occasional
     tumpty paraphrase of orchestration . . .
Largely indelibly . . . — yes: "The hills are alive . . .")

And still. Apt, for example, by the third chop on a
     carrot
to chime in or voice-over (show off? head off?) but
     senza voce,

"thwonk."

"Down in front!"

1. unmarred

On a torn scrap of paper on the weathered wood
of the porch to the overgrown yard, a worn 'g'—
since legible, <u>unmarred</u>.

. . . what doth the Lord require of thee?

"Aboard, aboard, for shame! The wind . . ."

                         Mrs. Larney assigned
"Polonius's advice to La-ray-tees" (we duly misread
     'Laertes')
and the Seventy Prepositions, rote.

"Aboard, about, above, across, after, against . . ."

The six dusts [perceptions], roots [senses] and
consciousnesses are originally empty.

"La-ray-tees."

A mockingbird, news and more news.

Portrait: his good-bye, its chaser upsip of breath.

And attending to listening, another listening.

Found yourself in the way of—encountered—(used up
    not much of it)
sound: a siren, birdsong, some truck or plane engine,
    snuck in (Danger:
yes, no?) not unlike suspicion—phase, duration—
    . . . *doth require thee?*

2. plaid

Writing in bed (the staff of an 'h' barely rose) when D.
    started a shower;
after countless rehearsals, "the sound of water"

                                        . . . with the thought
phrase (I thought I) made—not interference—an
    interference

pattern. <u>Plaid</u>. Played two duets.

CONVERSION (. QUIETLY)

When the mental "thwonk"s, my idiot sing-along,
     began—in this case I de-ended
(by overbending) spears of asparagus, so more like
     "snap"s: the overbearing, ideated
onomatopoeia—I played with (maneuver, subversion)
     reciting a phrase from a poem I'd been revising,
silently—but also quietly—repeating the phrase,
     "that same self-consciousness," "that same
     self-consciousness"
as mantra, work song; and, yes, there came—I heard—
     a fresh, interruptive (almost startling), fibrous
[snap!] each time a stem end broke off; that is, with
     the syllable 'same.'

VANTAGE

Either the well was very deep, or she fell very slowly, for she had plenty of time as she went down to look about her, and to wonder what was going to happen next.

LEWIS CARROLL, *ALICE'S ADVENTURES IN WONDERLAND*

POEM

Not thought, exactly: a refrain
of thought.

Standing by my bed

In gold sandals
Dawn that very
moment awoke me

—SAPPHO

I.

In it writing that
"the intervals"/*des in-*
tervalles

between color plates

provided by outsized (in it he explained "the
    exceptional size" of his) handwriting
were—

'whether or not you are reading this'?—

"PURELY VISUAL"/*LEUR RÔLE EST DONC
PUREMENT SPECTA-
CULAIRE.*

MATISSE, *JAZZ*

OR SHE FELL VERY SLOWLY

TAKE: DRIVING

through a pattern of girders and shadows

II. THE LAKE

In-
stead (noticing)—surrounding, and in eyes in, strokes
    and the hooked

inked marks of letters, of words—the fabric, the
    bleached
planche/rink, of paper: the page

that very moment (1/14/1997) that I'd been reading:
"There was the lake, barely visible through the trees."

\- - -

And again (4/15/1997) at:
"I heard the lake lapping softly against the rowboats
    tied to the dock."

GALLERY

MATISSE, *THE PIANO LESSON*

—"architectonic": I read that—the shadowed stage left
of his son's face, a précis inverting the shaft of green
(sunlight through a window) repeating the pyramid
   metronome.
He's not as young as he looks, the lad. *Tick, tock.*

MATISSE, *VIOLINIST AT THE WINDOW*

Self-portrait—his (half-rounded) back, for once,
blocking our view of the artist's view—'violinisting'. . .

PICASSO, *LES DEMOISELLES D'AVIGNON*

The artist's fear of them
so that the faces of some of the women came to
    resemble primitive masks—

frightening in their loose resemblance to human
    faces;
striking as the familiar, draped—

masks that were faces *between* ("against . . . ,
    intercesseurs, mediators": Picasso)

—yes, 'striking.'

VANTAGE

Here M. has painted the woman gazing, and
    background, her entire
surroundings . . .

(save himself and that [unsaved] half)—a thought.
Then again I 'come to.'

"She came to herself." (Before us.)

KOI

(I)

was doing my best to see them,
what with the reflection

KOAN

"Everyone knows the sound of two hands clapping.
What is the sound of one clapping hand?"

COINED

'Violinisting': coined. Then I leant on it.

The practice of *askew* until skewed feels like comfort
    ("a learned thing").

Restful? *Zzzz*—then I slept on it—sawed, a swaying
    (pitched), tuning fork, metronome . . .

awoke in the dark. Certainly electronic; I tried to
listen in triplets or randomness—*tick*, *tock*—the
lyric, based on a pendulum.

Not symmetrical, not ambidextrous, since I looked
over that way . . .

ADDED SAYINGS: KOAN

"Everyone knows the sound of two hands . . ." — (one
gloved?)
". . . clapping." — And startled, looks over (remember?)
"What is the sound of one clapping hand?" —

COINED

'Violinisting': I leant on it, changed. An instrument-
    closed loop.

(Melody, readied. A bow, drawn and drawn.)

Listen: whoever meant the melody once, I mean
    it now . . .

ADDED SAYINGS: COINED

'Violinisting': I leant on it, changed. — Can you read
    my thoughts?

An instrument-closed loop. (Melody, readied. — As
   yet without timbre.
A bow, drawn and drawn.) — *Shiver me timbers.*
Listen: whoever meant the melody once, I mean it
   now. — . . . my thoughts about 'unison thoughts'?

VANTAGE

As it happened I drowned the ants
on the plate to stop being God to them.

BACKSTORY

Not the action, itself . . . *Re:* I folded and put the letter
   in an envelope.

To trace, trace of—an intimacy:—reaching through the
   length
of the long legs of D.'s jeans to turn them inside out
   for laundering.

Handle—as object; role of the; its shadow.

[hand : envelope : letter : hand]

Action, once removed? (I refolded and returned the
   letter to its envelope.)

Then again, *mine* . . .

Her gift—"in return"—from the first decade of our
thirty-four-year correspondence, a selection of my
letters now 'returned to sender' carefully mounted in a
cord-tied, brocade-covered album, each in its opened,
original envelope. Various addresses, return addresses,
cancelled (5!- to 15-cent) stamps. Re-read with—Ver-
meer, maybe Hopper? Richter—fascinated apprehen-
sion, proceeding from (as Preface) a few notes from
high school "still" folded for passing and set—like the
envelopes—in photo corners: to unseat, unfold, hold
one for reading.

Portrait (artist's collection): his good-bye, its chaser
upsip of breath.

Action, haunting an 'itself.'

I put the letter (back) into an envelope.

USAGE

Home: your fully expecting to find x in a drawer.

"Slipped the track": or words to that effect.

You began speaking not even garbledly (overshot,
      worn-out),
still she was most encouraging.

Let y = once again y, instead of x.

Mother's milk, the transitional *apostrophe s*:
after all, put to your own uses.

"Kanzeon—(Japanese) Avalokitesvara; The One Who Perceives the Sounds of the World; incarnation of mercy and compassion"

Nor annoyed, I suppose, by my husband's—
    sporadically—noisy chewing.

DOOR

—shut:—the cries (which one can infer) have died out by here.

POOR USAGE

Drowned: combed-out fleas I tried calling 'blurry
   specks.'

HARBORED

And I (or: *And you*), responsible,

sole witness to the white latex glove—the sort
used these days for commercial food prep, restroom
    maintenance,
medical procedures which might result in the
    exchange of bodily fluids;
discarded—buoyed by the (with) cove down the rise,
    at a remove

but zoomed-in-on (in cartoons, the exchange of
    frame: cartoon eyes zoom-lensing out at,
in shock) in memory—*Close up: glove*—floating stately,
    plumply

supine (the Bay as right-handed), also cartoonishly
animate, quite Mickeyish, waving—locally—as though
   bidding

adieu to . . .

\- \- \-

And I (or: *And you*), World Honored One,

by a single sheet of an unclipped manuscript (was
   held, was read),
swept—gusts equalled swells—onto the fjord and,
   supine
(stanza shapes and four "corner words," for a time,
   discernible),

away: flexi- —equalled wavy—but surprisingly raftlike,
  making a sewing
(basting) motion, but less and less 'at hand,' also less
  intermittently
disappeared, with my- (*your-*) self—narrative thread—
  looking after with due

(—until?) expectation . . .

HORIZON: OLYMPIC RANGE,
WASHINGTON STATE, AUTUMN 1996

Life mask of George Washington (Morgan Library
    Exhibition catalog)
photographed in its case, in profile, supine (though
    bodiless);

the collection touring the States, our touring the
    displays.

Profile.

        I noticed I was
not content without picking out some feature of the
    landscape.

USES OF ITALICS

"Would the congregation please rise?"

                                    It . . . they
rose, some promptly,

some managing with a confiding—self-rallying?
    involuntary?—
'urgh'; some, on account of the prayerbook, even
    turning
to set a handkerchief or glasses case down on their
    (empty) seats,
".

    .

    .

—Now, joining me in the Responsive Reading:"—

So. 'Following' in the text: Rabbi's line (cue:),
worshipers' . . .

For three or four words at the outset, *All:*—most—
beginning reading to hear themselves [be heard]
among, to align;
                       some "setting the example,"
some slipping in "under cover of darkness" (i.e.,
     during a vowel, just skipping a first consonant),
     some hanging back
then pronouncing every word but hurriedly, to
     catch up—

becoming certain—(cue:), Rabbi's . . .

With italicized one-line opening stanzas

in "News Of: Codicils," "By the Pond," and "After
    Sappho,"
was (heretofore private) reference made to that period
    of courtship,
the more or less tentative many entrances of voices—

textured (as to the touch) and vibrant (as in hue)
as velvet trim with its mown lawn of tiny shadows.

To that; and to the single-line stanzas
heading each of Mary Barnard's Sappho translations
(lines enlisted as titles in the Contents)—invariably
    enjambed

phrases carrying the momentum of embarking—
    'underlined'
by brevity and isolation, their (momentary)

fragmentness

USES OF 'IT'

It could happen without warning.

It takes in the neighborhood of nine months.

It ran from me, its tether dangling.
No . . .

I was enjoying reading the (transcribed) talks of Zen
 Master Seung Sahn.
"*[Hits the table loudly.]*" it said. "*[Hits.]*"

It's no use

Mother dear, I
can't finish my
weaving
            You may
blame Aphrodite

soft as she is

she has almost
killed me . . .

                    —Sappho

USES OF I

distinguished—admired—the green white
flesh of the apple, the apple green

of its skin.

SELF-PORTRAIT (EROTICA)

Not only gasping but given voice.

STRIPPED

—to a pallor, and even some remnant of the white
    adhesive—

—to a pallor against which your forearms just matched
    the nipples—

—a pallor, yes, where ʾdoveʾ the lower pilings—

ERROR

Taking the handheld steamer for, the sake jar for
our modest "monument of cat" . . .

What to call: that for which something else is
    frequently mistaken?

At a very low tide, entire pilings: the lower halves or
    so, pale
—"with passion, Alice thought"—I thought, with being
(submerged) routinely 'played by' the reflected upper
    halves, exactly
waveringly shadowed over, overcast . . .

—" 'It's all her fancy, that' "— Seven uprights. Six
    pilings, one human figure

walking near the tideline. Seeing as half-seeing, half-
    reviewing: the 'fancy'
(that of poles half-entranced . . . -portrayed, as
    though entire . . .) coincident with vision
lighting on the beach stones—lightly: not much 'at' in
    it—"where I dream in my little hood with many
    bells /
jangling when I'd turn my head"—'post-traumatic'?—
    half-deep in reflection (a likeness
which woke me)—but I love (or, am loved) having
    caught my own . . . to savor
catching my harmless . . . oops—that version of
    pallor . . .

Of course, I'd lazed on the dock at the juncture—
wooden pilings half-sub/*bus-flah* (the '/merged,'
    obscured),
their treatment releasing its nacre to the water—
    saltwater

lapping and lapping, not correcting, feeding
the *acorn barnacles* (I looked up, later): little calcified
    volcanoes—'voracious slits'—
nearly contiguous up to the waterline, clinging to the
    pilings like lichen—
ashen . . .

SOME NOT

Like thoughts,
some become monuments.

ELEGY: ANNIVERSARY WALTZ

Error or trial and error, or trial? Were, mistakes were
   made.
'Stream of' relies on the simile . . . "sinewy" . . .
Heart once spelled threat once spelled treat, ten
   years dad.

– KARESANSUI –

"Ryōanji Temple, Kyōto; probably created 1499, when ridge-pole
of *hōjō* hall was put up. Flat dry-landscape garden *(karesansui)*
with stone arrangement in seven-five-three rhythm *(shichigosan)*
on white sand; cushions of moss have formed in the course of
time."

—IRMTRAUD SCHAARSCHMIDT-RICHTER AND OSAMU MORI,
 JAPANESE GARDENS

"Differ them photographs, plans lie:
how big it is!
austere a sea rectangular   of sand by the oiled mud wall,
and the sand is not quite white: granite sand, grey,

—from nowhere can one see *all* the stones—"

—JOHN BERRYMAN, FROM "DREAM SONG 73: *KARESANSUI, RYOAN-JI*" aboard about above across after against along amid amidst among amongst around at athwart before behind below beneath beside besides between betwixt beyond but by concerning considering despite down during ere except excepting for from in inside into like near notwithstanding of off on outside over past pending regarding respecting round save saving since through throughout till to toward towards under underneath unlike until unto up upon with within without

—THE SEVENTY PREPOSITIONS, ACCORDING TO MRS. LENORE LARNEY, APTOS JUNIOR HIGH SCHOOL, CA. 1962

NOTE: IN THE SUBTEXTS OF THE *KARESANSUI* POEMS, NUMBERS REFER
TO LINE NUMBER; UNATTRIBUTED SOURCES ARE BY THE AUTHOR.

"an ancient pond—
frog jumps in
the sound of water"

KARESANSUI

"an ancient pond" — lexicon — "with the thought/" —
"some not" — "As Syllable from" — "chosen and placed"

EPIGRAPH) MATSUO BASHŌ 1) BASHŌ; "TRACE" 2) "SOME NOT"; EMILY
DICKINSON, "[THE BRAIN—IS WIDER THAN THE SKY—]"; "FOR"

ABOUT

what one cannot face — "gets a look at those feet . . . "
   — *in extremis* —
back—defining/defining — "tuning fork,
   metronome" — " . . . and rushes back"

1) PROFESSOR WAGSTAFF (GROUCHO MARX) EXPLAINS BLOOD
CIRCULATION IN *HORSE FEATHERS*   2) "KOAN/COINED"; WAGSTAFF

AGAINST

wouldn't just anyone stiffen? — pressed — what must
   be a muzzle — instead of no — no

"A cloth, and I don't know if it's for a garment or for nothing."

leaning over the oysterbed, he looked — classic —
choosing among the existing —
"Crochet, souls, philosophy . . . " — approving/
murderous — moving about

AMONGST

EPIGRAPH, 2) FERNANDO PESSOA AS ALVARO DE CAMPOS,
"IMPASSIVELY"

BEFORE

shock of — ritual of entry — "Formality gave
   pleasure" — bequeathed — from the viewing
   platform,
stones I knew from their photographs! —
   unforeseeable: between

1) BRENDA HILLMAN, "CASCADIA"

BENEATH

particularly appreciative of the relatively flat: an
    expanse of water, ice rink, "dry-landscape garden
    (*karesansui*) with stone arrangement in seven-five-
    three rhythm (*shichigosan*) on white sand" — *once
    burned, twice shy* —
from childhood? — towering peaks, forget it

1) IRMSTRAUD SCHAARSCHMIDT-RICHTER AND OSAMU MORI, *JAPANESE
GARDENS*, CAPTION TO PLATE 17

BESIDE

"Or madly squeeze a right-hand foot
  Into a left-hand shoe"

"Compare and contrast." — sorrow of — insistent —
    beside —
kindness — it had been forever

EPIGRAPH) LEWIS CARROLL, "A-SITTING ON A GATE," *THROUGH
THE LOOKING-GLASS* 1) MAURICE F. ENGLANDER, ENGLISH EXAMS,
LOWELL HIGH SCHOOL

BETWEEN

repositioned on the loop — Self and Other —
-reliant — I foreswore (as companions)
objets — inert: *nature morte* — since our eyes met

" A coward dies a thousand deaths, the hero dies but one."

CONSIDERING

some act/experience resists description —
 'beggaring' — *a coward . . . a thousand . . .*
 — that which demanded a
'threshold language' — said of it: something held
 me back

EPIGRAPH) "COWARDS DIE MANY TIMES BEFORE THEIR DEATHS; / THE
VALIANT NEVER TASTE OF DEATH BUT ONCE." —WILLIAM SHAKESPEARE,
JULIUS CAESAR, ACT 2, SCENE 2

NEAR

at the root of listening — *hmmm* — not
   descriptive — waves —
near — "privilege of" — came in waves

2) JANE AUSTEN, *PRIDE AND PREJUDICE*, CHAPTER 8
(SEE "THROUGHOUT")

NOTWITHSTANDING

"*Amor fati* / The love of fate" — but *uh-oh* — will never
    know whether it would have been better to —
    missing —
so when the artist extends his thumb before the
    subject: what's that about? — what (could have)
    happened? — still missing — happened

1) GEORGE OPPEN, "OF BEING NUMEROUS"

OF

"I: Hints need the widest sphere in which to swing . . .
J: . . . where mortals go to and fro only slowly."

our — swing set swing — Ur of — invented perfecting

EPIGRAPH) MARTIN HEIDEGGER, "A DIALOG ON LANGUAGE"

REGARDING

"Still harping on that?" — 'harping' . . . each gesture, its
   retreat

,

" In order to attract the spirits and thus to participate in
their immortality, [Wu-ti] is reported to have
named rocky islands in a large pond or lake Islands
of Immortality or even to have created such
islands." — " 'He says he wants in his old age to be
surrounded by the work of his hands.' " — " 'Am I
addressing the White Queen?'
'Well, yes, if you call that a-dressing,' the Queen
said. 'It isn't *my* notion of the thing, at all.' "
— D. replied, "You have a strange way of putting
things."

SAVE

1) *RE* EMPEROR WU-TI (141–87 B.C.), IRMTRAUD SCHAARSCHMIDT-RICHTER AND OSAMU MORI, *JAPANESE GARDENS,* INTRODUCTION; CHAIM POTOK, *MY NAME IS ASHER LEV,* CHAPTER 8; LEWIS CARROLL, *THROUGH THE LOOKING-GLASS,* CHAPTER 5 2) CARROLL, CONTINUED; PRIVATE CONVERSATION (ARTIST'S COLLECTION)

SAVING

this small corner of planning — decor — 'though' —
   "little soap / / little / soap" — disaster photograph:
a doorframe left standing — just so —*personal void
   space* — [—] — for "Man be my metaphor"? . . . "Let
   this be my epitaph."

1) BRENDA HILLMAN, "CASCADIA" 2) *PERSONAL VOID SPACE:* AREA
PROTECTED FROM FALLING OBJECTS IN AN EARTHQUAKE (UNDER A
TABLE, FOR EXAMPLE); DYLAN THOMAS, "IF I WERE TICKLED BY THE RUB
OF LOVE"; SOURCE UNDETERMINED

THROUGH

would drive her for hours through neighborhoods to
    allay her panic — "(or pay for him / what he owes — "
    — At least there's
[?] — stripped — Charon — "at the Bone — " — " 'Can
    you take care of it now?' 'If not, there's no place
    to avoid.' "

1) STÉPHANE MALLARMÉ, *A TOMB FOR ANATOLE* (FRAGMENT 194)
2) EMILY DICKINSON, "[A NARROW FELLOW IN THE GRASS]"; THOMAS
CLEARY, TRANSLATOR, COMMENTARY TO CASE (KOAN) 87, "SUSHAN'S
'EXISTENCE AND NONEXISTENCE,'" *BOOK OF SERENITY*

"Chan Master Guangren of Sushan in Fukien called on
    Dongshan and asked, 'Please teach me the word
    that doesn't yet exist.' Dongshan said, 'When you
    don't consent, no one agrees.' Sushan said, 'Should
    one take care of it?' Dongshan said, 'Can you take
    care of it now?' Sushan said, 'If not, there's no
    place to avoid.' " — a continuum from eye to
    horizon,
including the eye ("that for me the space is one unity
    from the horizon to the interior of my work
    room") — "the whole of an afternoon" — " 'No one
    admitted to the privilege of hearing you, could
    think anything wanting.' "

THROUGHOUT

1) THOMAS CLEARY, TRANSLATOR, COMMENTARY TO CASE (KOAN) 87, "SUSHAN'S 'EXISTENCE AND NONEXISTENCE,'" *BOOK OF SERENITY;* HENRI MATISSE, PARAPHRASED FROM MEMORY 2) HENRI MATISSE, 1942 RADIO INTERVIEW, JACK FLAM, *MATISSE ON ART;* ROBERT HASS, "SANTA BARBARA ROAD"; JANE AUSTEN, *PRIDE AND PREJUDICE,* CHAPTER 8 (DARCY TO ELIZABETH BENNETT)

TO

would he take my photo: "Before" — up a path to the
    abbot's quarters—by train to Giverny —
    Auschwitz — site . . . "attraction" —
preserved the ticket — the very shoes

TOWARD

obstruction and its opposite —*is*— the view

WITH

skimming Feynman for the passage proposing
   light is emitted only in response to a perceiving
   instrument — 'nudged' — along the margin
by Heisenberg's Principle of Uncertainty (in the tiny,
   tidy, serif hand of my early twenties): "as one
   changes the self by self-knowledge?" — "swayed . . .
   O brightening glance . . ."

2) WILLIAM BUTLER YEATS, "AMONG SCHOOLCHILDREN"

WITHOUT

"That it should come to this" — "the fifteen changeless
    stones in their five worlds / . . . of the ancient
    maker priest" — as Rembrandt [showed us he]
knew he'd become paint — that it should

1) WILLIAM SHAKESPEARE, *HAMLET,* ACT 1, SCENE 2; JOHN BERRYMAN,
"DREAM SONG 73: *KARESANSUI, RYOAN-JI"*

" The way the drowned leave their names above water."

RYŌAN-JI

framed, yet — dry, yet — the gravel, its
rakedness — "how big it is!" — reminiscent, yet

EPIGRAPH) LAURA MULLEN, "SESTINA IN WHICH MY GRANDMOTHER
IS GOING DEAF" 2) JOHN BERRYMAN, "DREAM SONG 73: *KARESANSUI,
RYOAN-JI*"

NOTES

VOCABULARY SENTENCES: PART EPIGRAPH
"So, before I could go on," from " 'The Story of a Terrible Brain
Injury,' " A. R. Luria, *The Man with a Shattered World*, translated
by Lynn Solotaroff, foreword by Oliver Sacks (Cambridge, Mass.:
Harvard University Press, 1987).

BIT
"the extreme verge," William Shakespeare, *King Lear*, act 4, scene
6; "a certain Slant of," Emily Dickinson, "[There's a certain Slant
of light]," *The Poems of Emily Dickinson*, edited by Thomas H.
Johnson (Cambridge, Mass.: Harvard University Press, 1983).

ALSO TO ILLUSTRATE
Excerpts from the diaries of L. Zaseysky from "On Recollect-
ing Words *(The Second Digression)*" and " 'My World Has No

Memories,'" Luria, *Man with a Shattered World;* "I tried to say to," Stevie Smith in a letter, from *Stevie Smith: A Biography* by Frances Spaulding (New York: Norton, 1989).

TRACE

"The hills are alive," lyric excerpt from "The Sound of Music" by Richard Rodgers and Oscar Hammerstein II; "what doth the Lord," Micah 6:8; "Aboard, aboard, for shame!" William Shakespeare, *Hamlet,* act 1, scene 3; "The six dusts," "Just-Like-This Is Buddha," after Pai Chang, Zen Master Seung Sahn, *The Compass of Zen* (Boston and London: Shambhala, 1997); "the sound of water," Matsuo Bashō: "an ancient pond — / frog jumps in / the sound of water," translation adapted by Carol Snow from Hiroaki Sato, *One Hundred Frogs: From Renga to Haiku to English* (New York and Tokyo: John Weatherhill, 1983).

VANTAGE: PART EPIGRAPH

Lewis Carroll, *Alice's Adventures in Wonderland* (New York: Penguin, 1998), chapter 1.

JAZZ/THE LAKE

"Standing by my bed," Sappho, from *Sappho: A New Translation,* translated by Mary Barnard (Berkeley and Los Angeles: University of California Press, 1958); "*LEUR RÔLE,*" Henri Matisse, *Jazz* (New York: Braziller, 1985); "There was the lake," Chaim Potok, *The Book of Lights* (New York: Knopf, 1981), chapter 10; "I heard the lake," Chaim Potok, *The Gift of Asher Lev* (New York: Knopf, 1990), chapter 7.

GALLERY

"*intercesseurs,* mediators," Picasso to André Malraux as quoted in *Picasso: Creator and Destroyer,* Arianna Stassinopoulos Huffington (New York: Simon & Schuster, 1988), chapter 3.

KOAN/COINED

The "Added Sayings" form is after *Book of Serenity,* translated by Thomas Cleary (Hudson, N.Y.: Lindesfarne Press, 1990). "Everyone knows," Zen Master Hakuin (1686–1768), possibly more correctly, "What is the sound of one hand?"; "a learned thing," Carol Snow, "Positions of the Body," *Artist and Model* (New York: Atlantic Monthly Press, 1990).

BACKSTORY

For Kathleen Rendon Hirschfeld.

DOOR

"Kanzeon," found in a glossary of Buddhist terms,
www.Buddhanet.net, Buddha Dharma Education Association.

HARBORED

For Brenda Hillman. See "A Geology," Brenda Hillman, *Cascadia*
(Middletown, Conn.: Wesleyan University Press, 2001).

USES OF ITALICS

"News Of: Codicils," "By the Pond," and "After Sappho," Carol
Snow, *For* (Berkeley and Los Angeles: University of California
Press, 2000); "It ran from me," from "Tether," *ibid.; "[Hits the
table loudly.],* " Seung Sahn, *Compass of Zen;* "It's no use," Sappho,
translated by Barnard, *Sappho: A New Translation.*

ERROR

"monument of cat," Wallace Stevens, "A Rabbit As King of the
Ghosts," *The Palm at the End of the Mind: Selected Poems and a
Play by Wallace Stevens,* edited by Holly Stevens (New York: Knopf,
1971); "with passion, Alice thought" and " 'It's all her fancy, that,' "
Carroll, *Alice's Adventures in Wonderland,* chapters 2 and 9; "where
I dream in my little hood," Robert Duncan, " 'My Mother Would

Be a Falconress,'" *Bending the Bow*, reprinted in *Selected Poems* (New York: New Directions, 1993).

ELEGY: ANNIVERSARY WALTZ

For Sanford Snow. "sinewy," Robert Hass, "Interrupted Meditation," *Human Wishes* (New York: Ecco Press, 1989).

—*KARESANSUI*—: PART EPIGRAPHS

Irmtraud Schaarschmidt-Richter and Osamu Mori, introduction to *Japanese Gardens*, English translation by Janet Seligman (New York: Morrow, 1979), caption to plate 17; excerpt from "Dream Song 73: *Karesansui, Ryoan-ji*," by John Berryman, *The Dream Songs* (New York: Farrar, Straus & Giroux, 1959).

KARESANSUI

"an ancient pond," Bashō, translated by Snow after Sato, *One Hundred Frogs*; "with the thought," Snow from "Trace," *The Seventy Prepositions*; "As Syllable from" from "[The Brain — is wider than the Sky —]," Dickinson, *Poems*; "chosen and placed," Snow, "For" in *For*.

ABOUT

"The blood rushes from the head down to the feet, gets a look at those feet, and rushes back to the head again," Professor Wagstaff (Groucho Marx) in *Horse Feathers*, directed by Norman Z. McLeod, 1932.

AMONGST

"A cloth" and "crochet, souls, philosophy" from "Impassively," Fernando Pessoa as Alvaro de Campos, *Pessoa & Co.*, translated by Richard Zenith (New York: Grove Press, 1998).

BEFORE

"Formality gave pleasure," Hillman, "Cascadia," *Cascadia*.

BENEATH

"dry-landscape garden *(karesansui),*" Schaarschmidt-Richter and Mori, caption to plate 17, *Japanese Gardens*.

BESIDE

"Or madly squeeze," Lewis Carroll, "A-sitting On A Gate," *Through the Looking-Glass*, chapter 8.

CONSIDERING

"Cowards die many times," William Shakespeare, *Julius Caesar,*
act 2, scene 2.

NEAR

"privilege of," Jane Austen, *Pride and Prejudice* (Oxford, New York:
Oxford University Press, 1999), chapter 8.

NOTWITHSTANDING

"*Amor fati,* " George Oppen, "Of Being Numerous," *New Collected
Poems* (New York: New Directions, 2002).

OF

"I: Hints need," Martin Heidegger, "A Dialog on Language,"
translated by Peter D. Hertz, in *On the Way to Language* (New York:
Harper & Row, 1971).

SAVE

"In order to attract," Schaarschmidt-Richter and Mori, *Japanese
Gardens;* " 'He says he wants," Chaim Potok, *My Name Is Asher Lev*
(New York: Knopf, 1972), chapter 8; " 'Am I addressing," Carroll,
Through the Looking-Glass, chapter 5.

SAVING

"little soap," Hillman, "Cascadia"; "Man be my metaphor," Dylan
Thomas, "If I were tickled by the rub of love," *The Collected Poems
of Dylan Thomas 1934–1952* (New York: New Directions, 1971).

THROUGH

For Adrienne. "(or pay for him," Stéphane Mallarmé, fragment
194, *A Tomb for Anatole,* translated by Paul Auster (San Francisco:
North Point Press, 1983); "at the Bone" from "[A Narrow Fellow in
the Grass]," Dickinson, *Poems;* "Can you take," Case 87 in Cleary,
Book of Serenity.

THROUGHOUT

"Chan Master Guangren," Case 87 in Cleary, *Book of Serenity;*
"(that for me," Henri Matisse, "Radio Interview 1942," Jack Flam,
Matisse on Art (Berkeley and Los Angeles: University of California
Press, 1995); "the whole of an afternoon," from "Santa Barbara
Road," Hass, *Human Wishes;* "'No one admitted," Austen, *Pride and
Prejudice,* chapter 8.

TO

For Elizabeth Abel.

WITH

For Linda Norton. "swayed . . . ," William Butler Yeats, "Among Schoolchildren," *Selected Poems and Two Plays of William Butler Yeats*, edited by M. L. Rosenthal (New York: Macmillan, 1962).

WITHOUT

"That it should come," William Shakespeare, *Hamlet*, act 1, scene 2; "the fifteen changeless stones," from "Dream Song 73: *Karesansui, Ryoan-ji*," Berryman, *Dream Songs*.

RYŌAN-JI

"The way the drowned," Laura Mullen, "Sestina in Which My Grandmother Is Going Deaf," *The Surface* (Urbana and Chicago: University of Illinois Press, 1991); "how big it is!" Berryman, "Dream Song 73: *Karesansui, Ryoan-ji*."

ACKNOWLEDGMENTS

Sincere thanks to the editors of the following journals, where versions of some of these poems first appeared:

DENVER QUARTERLY
FIVE FINGERS REVIEW
FOURTEEN HILLS (THE SAN FRANCISCO STATE UNIVERSITY REVIEW)
MARY
NEW AMERICAN WRITING
POETRY FLASH
SYLLOGISM
VOLT
XANTIPPE

With gratitude to—and for—the readers, particularly first readers Patricia Dienstfrey, Brenda Hillman, and Laura Mullen. My thanks to Joan Landsberg, fellow memorizer, for her art; to Denise Newman for the first koan and a crucial suggestion. And to David Matchett.

ACKNOWLEDGMENTS
OF PERMISSIONS

TEXT: Filosofia
DISPLAY: Interstate
DESIGNER: Jessica Grunwald
COMPOSITOR: G&S Typesetters, Inc.
PRINTER AND BINDER: Friesens Corporation